Picture This! Animals

ARCTURUS

ARCTURUS

This edition published in 2023 by Arcturus Publishing Limited
26/27 Bickels Yard, 151–153 Bermondsey Street,
London SE1 3HA

Copyright © Arcturus Holdings Limited

All rights reserved. No part of this publication may be reproduced, stored in a
retrieval system, or transmitted, in any form or by any means, electronic, mechanical,
photocopying, recording, or otherwise, without prior written permission in accordance
with the provisions of the Copyright Act 1956 (as amended). Any person or persons
who do any unauthorized act in relation to this publication may be liable to criminal
prosecution and civil claims for damages.

Author: William Potter
Illustrator: Gareth Conway
Editor: Violet Peto
Designer: Stefan Holliland
Managing Editor: Joe Harris

ISBN: 978-1-3988-1531-5
CH010113NT
Supplier 29, Date 0123, PI 00002161

Printed in China

Unleash your imagination by transforming everyday objects into unexpected animals. From a pasta jellyfish to a pear polar bear, there are plenty of madcap ideas and suggestions to spark your creativity.

Pencil and Paper Pals

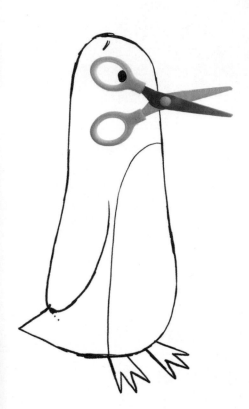

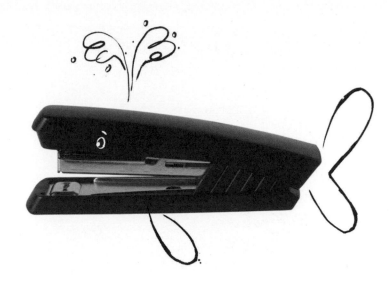

Have a whale of a time
with this stapler.

5

Back to Your Roots

What will you
dig up today?

Give this sausage dog
a plump pooch pal.

Turn this ravishing
radish into a proud
peacock with a fancy tail.

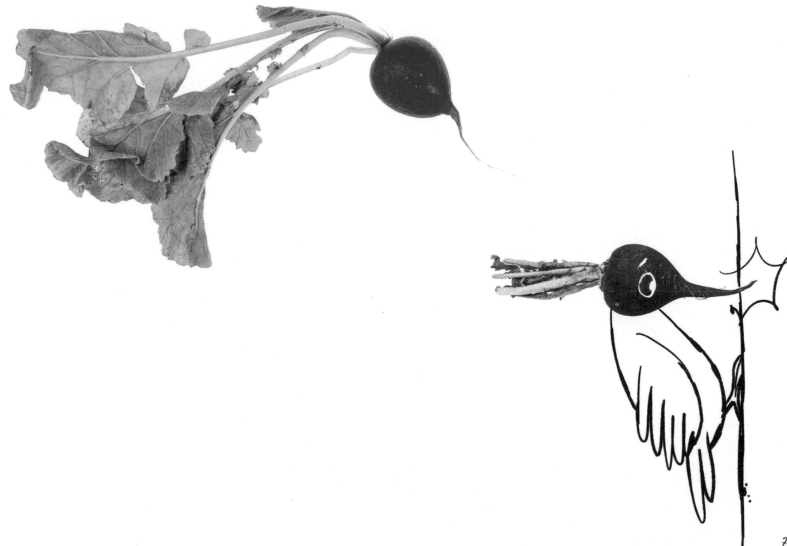

Triassic Toolbox

Try a Triceratops with a
staple gun for the beak
and horn.

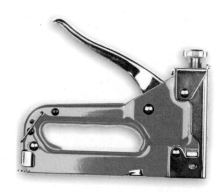

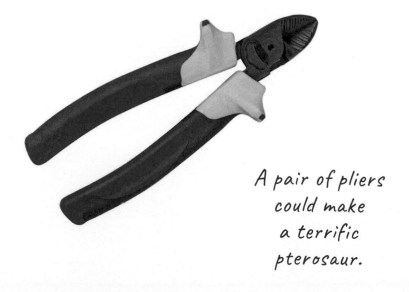

A pair of pliers
could make
a terrific
pterosaur.

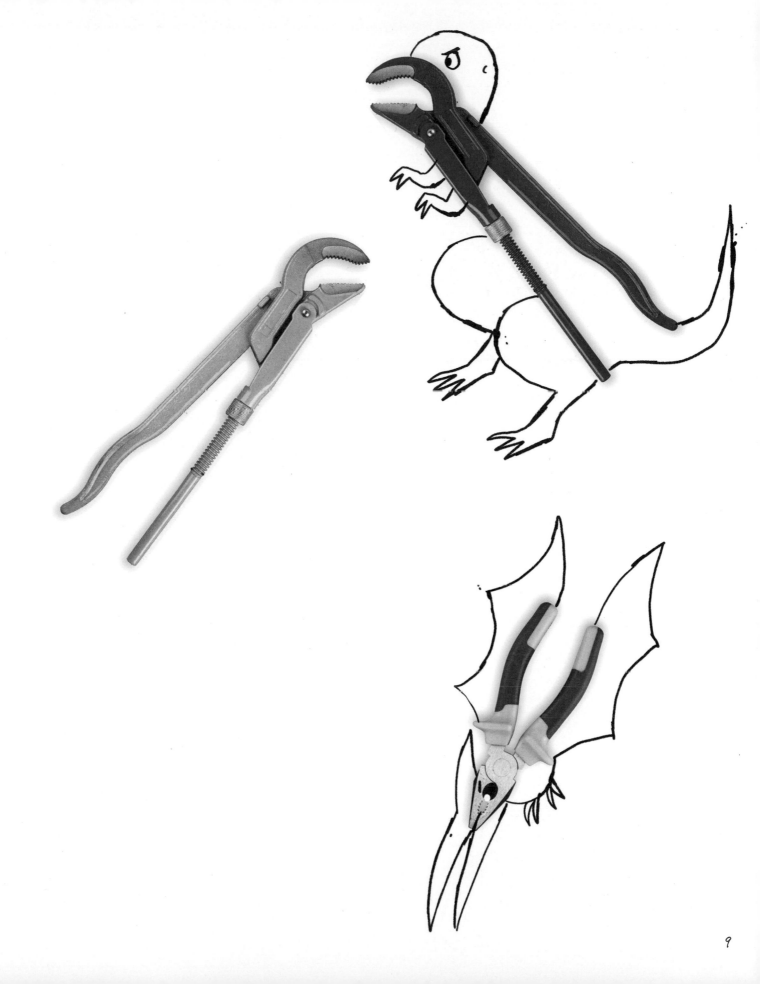

Spiky Surprises

What prickly pictures
will you come up with?

This exotic bird has
a spiny crest.

Wild and Woolly

Knit yourself
some yarn
creatures.

Add ears and a
whiskery snout to
make a chubby mouse.

Slice of Life

Turn this strawberry into
a beautiful bug by adding
wings and big black spots.

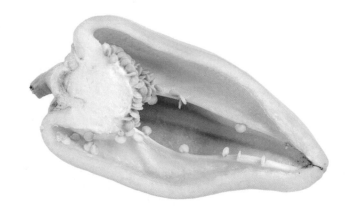

Why not turn
this lemon
slice into a
pelican pouch?

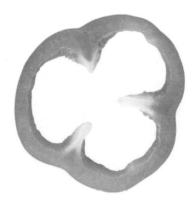

Open wide! A great
white shark shows
off its teeth.

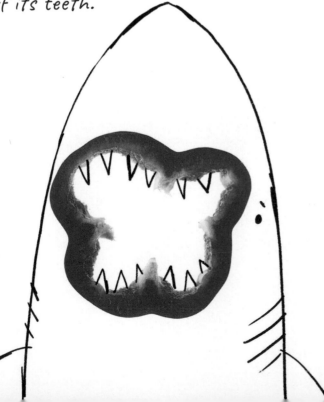

Beany Beasts

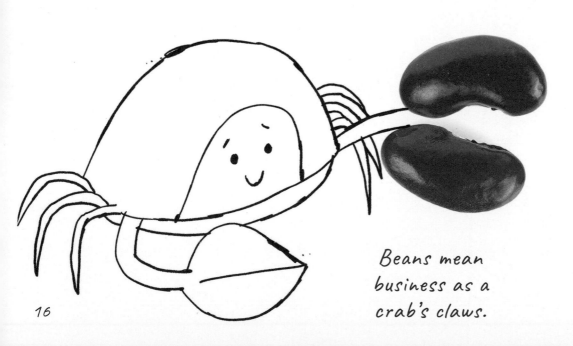

Beans mean
business as a
crab's claws.

Could a bean be
a tufty tail for
a squirrel?

Add webbed feet and a bill
for a playful platypus.

Tied Up

Don't get in a tangle doodling over these knots.

Give this
loop some
long ears,
and you've
got a rabbit!

Bird, fish, or reptile?
You decide!

Kitchen Creatures

What's cooking in the kitchen?

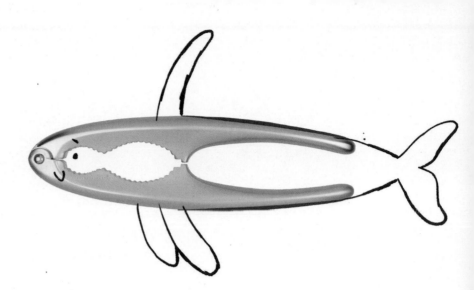

A rolling pin tops a sheep.

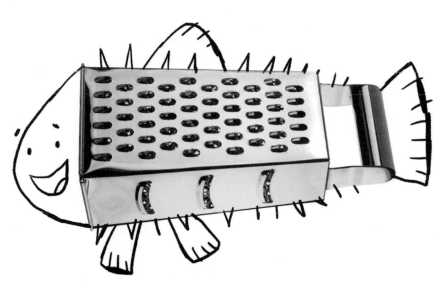

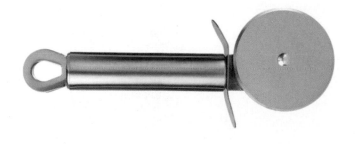

This pizza cutter already has fins. Give it a tail and head to turn it into a fearsome fish.

Merry Berries

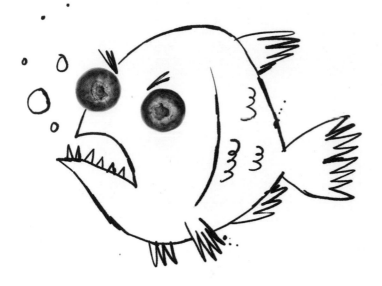

What critters can you
make from berries?

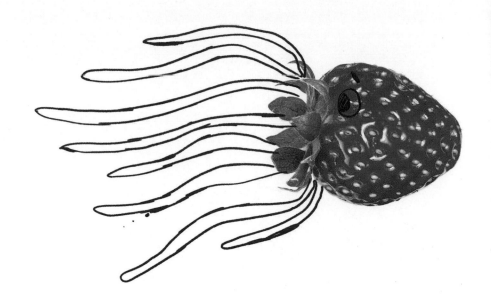

Add long tentacles
to make a
squirming squid.

Beach Life

Turn this towel into a manta ray!

Beachwear
or wings for
a macaw?

Say Cheese!

What cheesy critters can you come up with?

A chunk of cheese could be a body or a beak.

Super Scoops

What cool creatures will
you shape from ice cream?

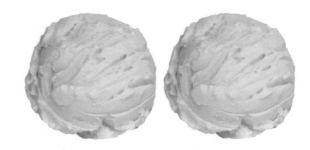

Two scoops for a
Bactrian camel.

Make this frozen
treat into a cool cat.

Chunky Chocs

Chocolates in line make the perfect segmented insect body.

What a stink! Who left
these behind?!

Desk Dwellers

Get down to business and doodle something wild!

Turn this tasty
snack into a
lobster body.

Doodle a dolphin with a key for a snout.

A Brush with Greatness

Turn brushes into animals,
and groom their coats.

A comb could become a condor's outstretched wings.

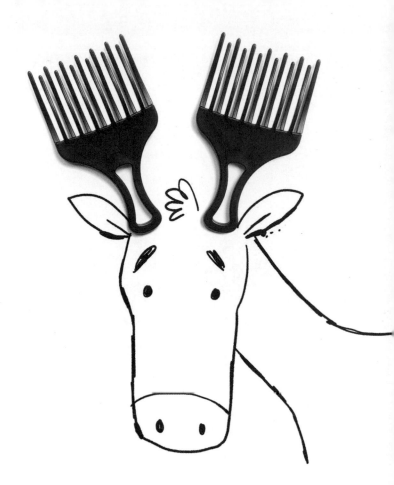

A jumbo jellyfish has lots of stingers.

Leafy Lines

Turn over a new leaf with
these wild animals.

Try turning a lovely leaf into an
exotic head crest, an insect body,
or a fan of tail feathers.

Baked Beings

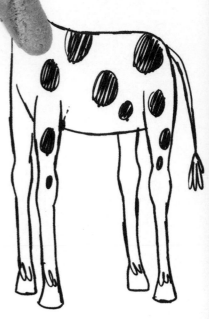

A baguette can make a giraffe's long neck.

What crusty creatures will you bake?

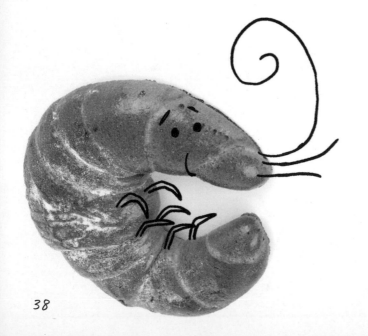

This nutty loaf would make
the perfect armadillo!

Best Blooms

Arrange these flowers into fantastic creatures.

A bright, yellow flower could become a fluffy chick.

A lovely lily
makes a hovering
hummingbird.

Vivid Vases

What wonders will
you shape from vases?

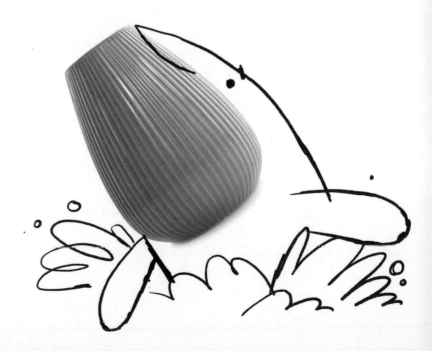

A wide-bottomed vase matches a spoonbill beak.

On the Ball

Can you bounce ideas off these balls?

A pair of
baseballs
could become
beady eyes.

Crumbly Creatures

Create some cool critters from cookies.

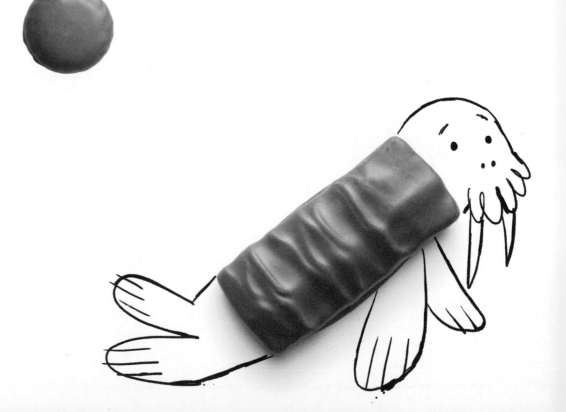

A cookie meerkat stands to attention.

Chew on This!

Make these gummy
candies come alive!

Spots and legs
turn this lozenge
into a lovely bug.

Hiss! A gummy worm
becomes a spitting
cobra.

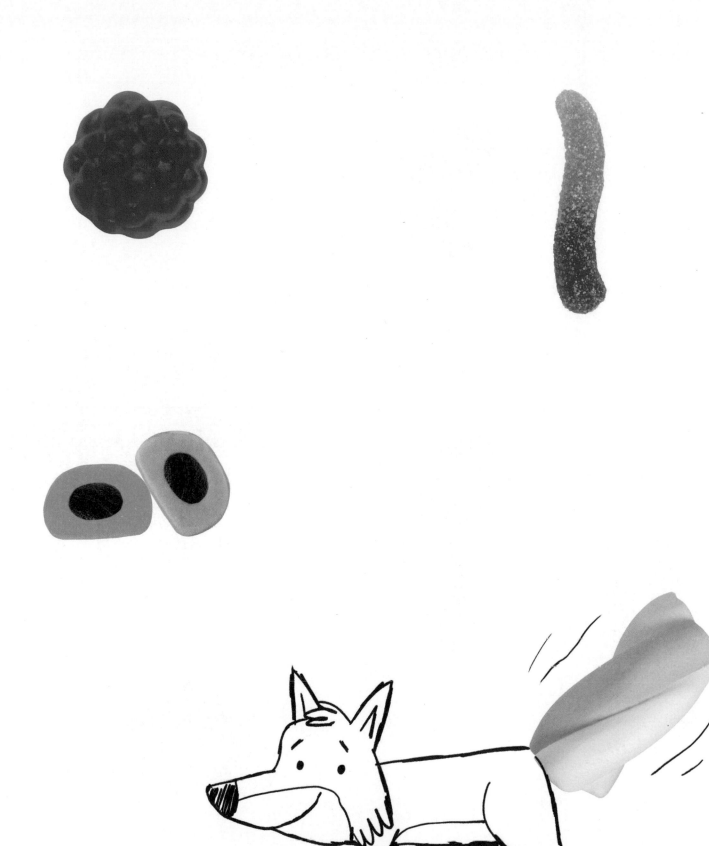

Wild Wigs

What furry
creatures could be
hiding in this hair?

Try turning this wig
of curls into a shaggy
sheep's fleece.

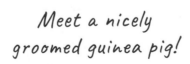

Meet a nicely groomed guinea pig!

Nutty Nature

Keep on creating creatures!

A curly cashew could be a hooked bird beak.

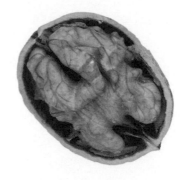

Could this be a
bug with a sting?

Nuts and Bolts

Turn a bolt into a
hammerhead shark!

Turn a pair of nuts
into panda eyes.

A screw becomes
a twisting
narwhal tusk.

Cutlery Creations

Serve up some wildlife with knives, forks, and spoons.

Help support an ostrich with a pair of knives.

Two spoons, or
dragonfly wings?

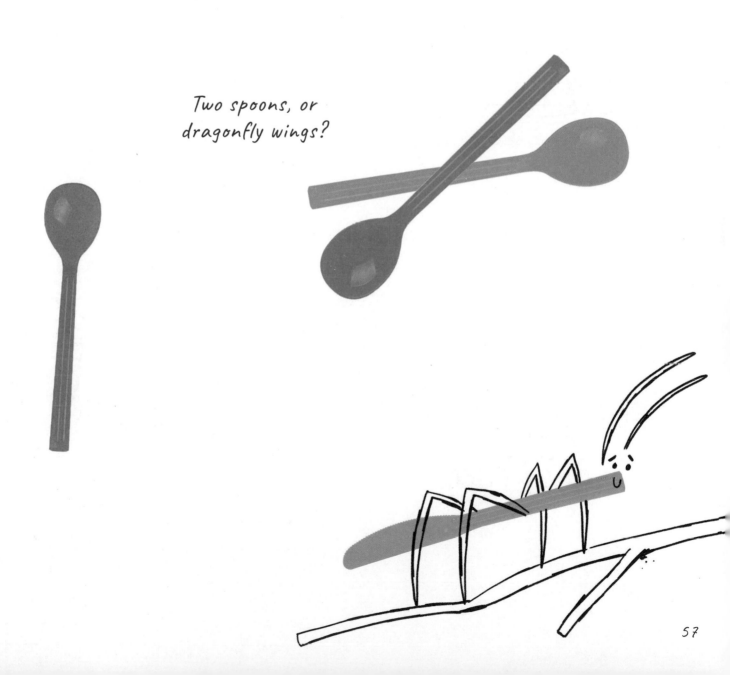

Creature Clips

Listen up! Paper clips could be bunny ears.

Two pushpins make antlers for a young deer.

Could this be a
snapping croc?

Bottle Tops

What wildlife can you squeeze from these bottles?

This bottle is truly jumbo!.

A curved bottle neck could be a beak or a trunk.

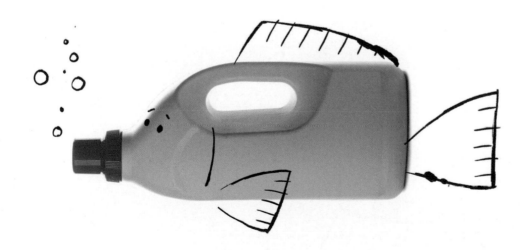

Clever Closet

Dress up these clothes
as animals!

Try making this shoe
into a rhino horn!

A fish in a skirt or a
trout with a tail?

Dumpling Doodles

What will you dish up with these dumplings?

A dumpling makes a full belly for a fowl.

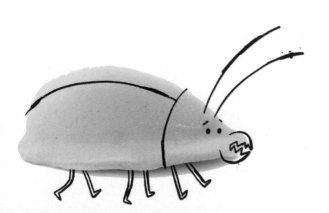

Could these dumplings
be folded wings?

Tangerine Town

Boing! It's a leaping jerboa.

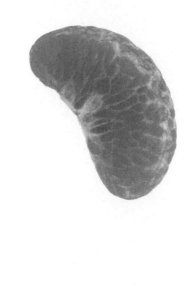

Could this be a
fruity bird bill?

Two segments
make a clawsome
lobster.

Shell Shapes

Shh, or you'll wake this snoozing dormouse.

The armadillo has
a tough exterior.

Sock It to Me!

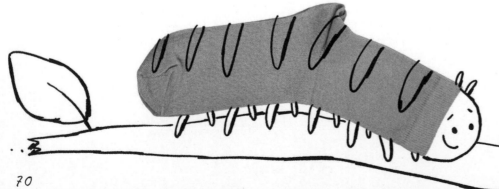

A green sock or a greedy caterpillar?

The Tasmanian devil has a sock collar.

Antlers or antennae? You decide!

Wild Wood

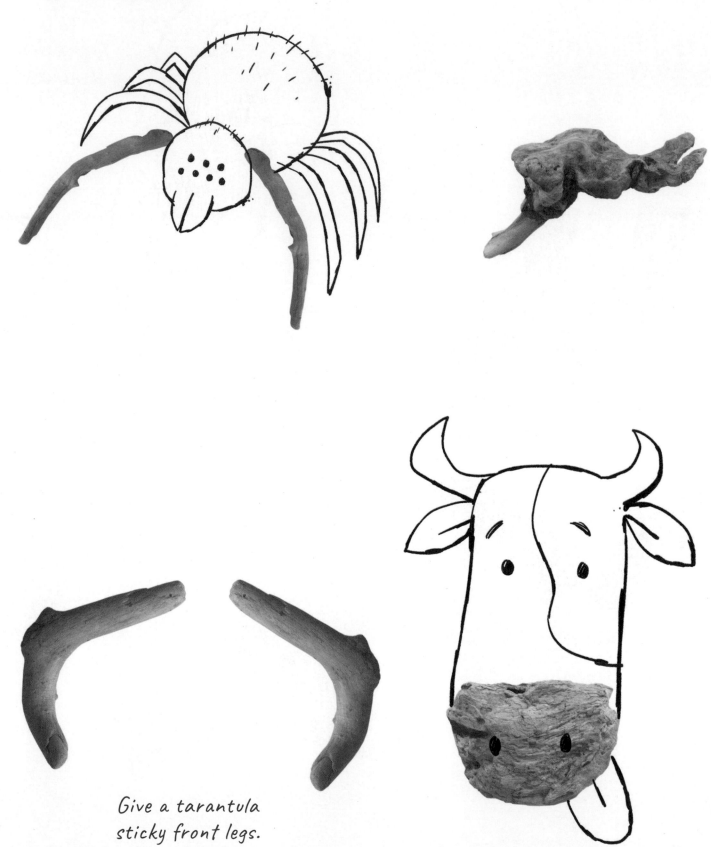

Give a tarantula
sticky front legs.

A wooden beak is
something to crow about.

Petal Pictures

Help these petals grow
into wild animals.

Two petal wings lift
a moth into the air.

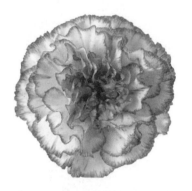

Could this be a
Triceratops' frill?

Crafty Caps

A bottle cap can make a face for a perky puffin.

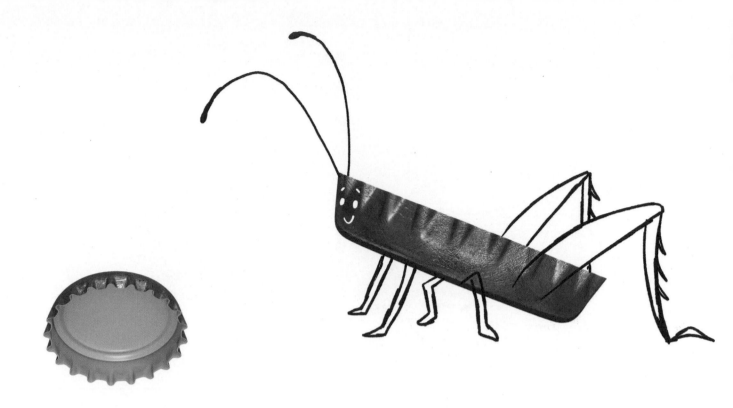

Whose eyes could
these be?

Mitten Magic

A mitten thumb
makes the jaw of a
mighty sperm whale.

Two mitts make
perfect paws for
an otter.

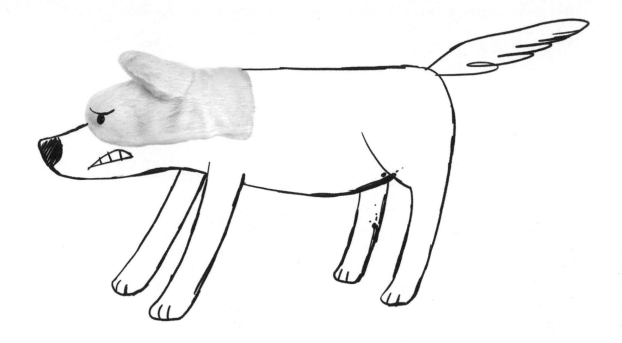

A fan made of mittens? Or a display of tail feathers?

Creature Count

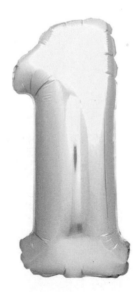

There's a buzz about this number eight.

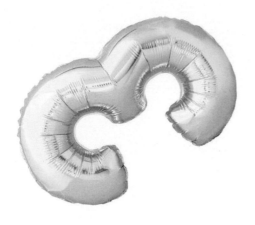

A fishy number nine.

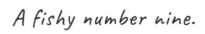

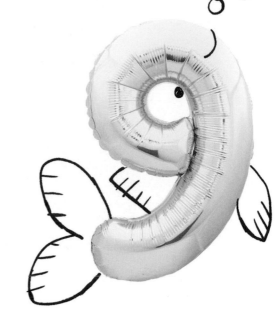

Go Bananas!

What a-peeling creatures will you design?

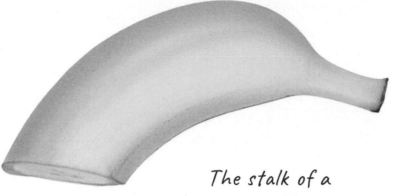

The stalk of a banana could make a dolphin's nose.

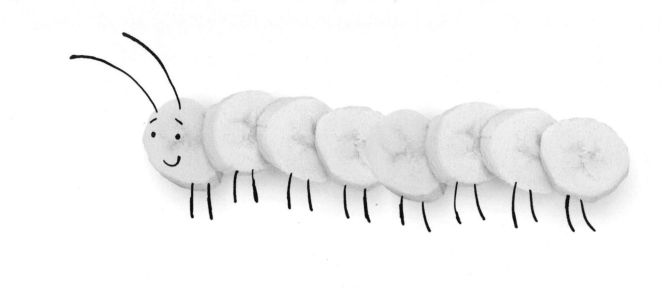

This proboscis monkey smells bananas!

Looking Sharp

Add animal magic to
these arrowheads.

A Stone Age arrow or
a cute koala nose?

Brushstrokes

Add creature features
to the paint smears.

This flying fish is
making a splash.

Cork Critters

Change corks into cool creatures.

Why not pop this cork onto a duck's body?

Could a cork
become a long
snout?

Carrot Chops

Carrot sticks or
echidna spikes?

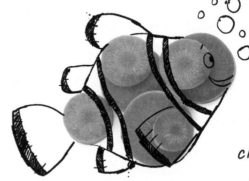

The cute
clownfish has
orange and
white stripes.

Grated carrots
or rooster
plumage?

Under Your Nose

Add fake facial
hair to your
animal pictures.

The nimble
gazelle has a
racing stripe.

This stylish 'tache is perfect for falcon wings.

Deep-Sea Pasta

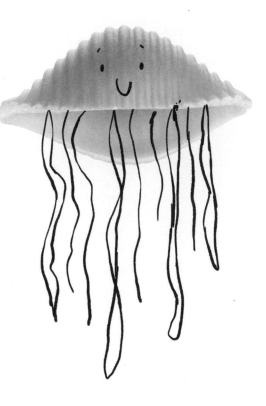

What sea creatures
do these pasta shapes
remind you of?

Could this
be a slinky
seahorse?

Pasta shells make
perfect fish.

Creative Creatures

Let your imagination run wild, and turn
these pictures into any animals you like!